Butterfly Blessings

Butterflies

Butterflies are different and quite unique,
for when they start out, they are ugly as can be.

They hide in a cocoon many days and nights.
Then when they come out, what a beautiful sight.

Butterflies are in one way similar to you and me;
we all chose our way of life,
but not the color that we will be.

The next glance of a butterfly,
please do not think of others.
We all are from the same creator,
yet we are all different colors.

All butterflies are not identical,
there are no two the same.
God made them on purpose,
Adam gave them their name.

No matter if you are average, purple, black or white.
Just like the butterfly, God made you just right.

-**Arethea M. Green**

Butterfly Blessings

Arethea Martin Green

Copyright

Copyright © 2016 by Arethea Martin Green. All rights reserved. This book or any portion thereof may not be reproduced or used in any manner whatsoever without the express written permission of The Butterfly Typeface Publishing House Co. except for the use of brief quotations in a book review.

Printed in the United States of America

First Printing, 2016

ISBN-13: 978-1-942022-57-2

The Butterfly Typeface Publishing
PO BOX 56193
Little Rock, Arkansas 72215

Dedication

II Corinthians 3:5 Not that we are sufficient of ourselves to think anything as of ourselves; but our sufficiency is of God;

Therefore, this book is dedicated to the Lord God my Saviour, the one that created me, saved me, and strengthens me. To Him and Him alone do I owe "All" for He has done great things for me and I am forever grateful.

When we extend love towards those that hate us as Christians, God says that we are blessed.

Being hated and seeing others hated can be a spiritual challenge, the Lord is concerned with all that we experience in life. He certainly has a reward for our hardships that we endure.

"Therefore, my beloved brethren,
be ye stedfast, unmoveable,
always abounding in the work of the Lord,
forasmuch as ye know
that your labour is not in vain in the Lord."

-Corinthians 15:58

Contents

His Mercies Are Still New 17
Sometimes We Are Empty 22
Teachers of Good Things 28
What Does God Say About Children? 35
Good Friendships and Out of Date Calendars 42
The "To Do" List 46
America, Our Veterans Need Us! 53
Arguing for Nothing 59
Things We Say When We Are Hurting 64
Waiting On Your Next Journey 69
The Virtuous, Nagging Woman 74
Things That Stink! 78
Living In A Manhole 85
Let's Just Stop Fooling Ourselves 90
We Will Always Have Haters 96
Faith During A Funeral 100
An Earthly Goodbye 107
The End 108
Butterfly Beginnings Book Reviews 109
A Note to My Momma 114
Thank You 115
About the Author 117

Foreword

When I lived in North Carolina, God had me on a path where I had to learn resilience, to lean on Him and patience. It was a lot to say the least and just when I was about to give up and throw in the towel, He sent me a friend.

She had no motives or intentions – she simply showed up and did what He sent her to do. Every visit was better than the one before and for hours we spoke about everything and nothing and in those times I learned to value life, family, friendship and love.

Along with several others in North Carolina, Arethea showed me what it meant to serve God with your heart rather than your understanding.

I'm a better woman, mother and friend because of her. She truly is a God send and every word she speaks and writes feels as if it's straight from His heart to mine.

I know you will feel the same.

I love you Arethea. Thank you for allowing Him to use you! Some may say it has been a long time coming, but for me you were right on time!

Iris M Williams

Acknowledgement

To everyone who took the time purchase and read my first book, Butterfly Beginnings; your support and encouragement propelled and inspired me to write this book. I pray it too will be a blessing.

-**Arethea Martin Green**

Introduction

What You Should Find Within This Devotional

It is my desire that you would find Jesus written of and described through some of my valley and mountain top experiences in life. With all of my heart I desire to love and gain a closer walk with the Lord on a daily basis. You should hear echo's within the pages of His undying love for us and also of His "Saving Grace". No one is perfect, that is why Jesus accepts us just as we are, with the intentions of us trusting Him as our Lord and Saviour. His blood washes away our sins and as we follow Him we are transformed into His image.

Within this devotional, I also hope that you would perhaps see a little of yourself within the scriptures and it causes you to be drawn closer to Him and the peace that He desires us all to have. There will be a space provided for you to journal and jot down a prayer request. More than anything I pray that you end your reading knowing that the Lord Jesus Christ has an everlasting, unconditional love for us all.

Jeremiah 31:3 The Lord hath appeared of old unto me, saying, Yea, I have loved thee with an everlasting love: therefore with lovingkindness have I drawn thee.

May God be all that you need and trust in this life from day to day.

"Because He Lives" Corinthians 15:58

Chapter One

His Mercies Are Still New

*L**amentations 3:22-23** It is of the Lord's mercies that we are not consumed, because his compassions fail not. They are new every morning: great is thy faithfulness.*

As old as the Bible is, God's words are as new as the mornings. It is as current as the day that He inspired it. It needs not to be re-written, only re-read. In this time in which we live, with all that is going on across America and other countries; His mercies are still new.

Psalm 119:64 *The earth, O Lord, is full of thy mercy: teach me thy statutes.*

Monday, Tuesday and all of the other days of the week will always be as different as their names. God constantly provides us with new blessings, because His mercies are new each day.

Psalm 23:6 *Surely goodness and "mercy" shall follow me all of the days of my life: and I will dwell in the house of the Lord forever.*

During times in our lives when we are at our lowest, His mercies are still new.

Psalm 27:7 *Hear O Lord, when I cry with my voice: have "mercy" also upon me, and answer me.*

When it appears that the world has forsaken us, His mercies are still new.

Psalm 30:10 *Hear, O Lord, and have "mercy" upon me: Lord, be thou my helper.*

When the doctors have given up on us or that loved one, be encouraged because His mercies are still new.

Psalm 31:7 *I will be glad and rejoice in thy "mercy": for thou hast considered my trouble; thou hast known my soul in adversities;*

When our work environment is more than we can handle from day to day, keep trusting because His mercies are new.

Psalm 31:9 *Have "mercy" upon me, O Lord, for I am in trouble: mine eye is consumed with grief, yea, my soul and my belly.*

When the child that we have raised through the church and prayed so much for breaks our heart we keep praying because His mercies are still new.

Psalm 103:17 *But the "mercy" of the Lord is from everlasting to everlasting upon them that fear him, and his righteousness unto children's children;*

When our home and/or marriage that once stood strong for the Lord begins to fail; never give up. His mercies are still new.

Psalm 33:22 *Let thou "mercy" O Lord, be upon us, according as we hope in thee.*

When we all often struggle with things that we know that we should not be doing, it is then that we should call on Jesus, because His mercies are still new.

Psalm 66:20 *Blessed be God, which hath not turned away my prayers, nor his "mercy" from me.*

It can be very hard to accept and believe sometimes, that tomorrow the Lord will deliver unto us new mercies for that day.

Psalm 90:14 *O satisfy us early with thy "mercy" that we may rejoice and be glad all our days.*

We often become so consumed with the worries of the present that we pull along today's troubles into the next day. We must remember that even if the troubles remain, new mercies are there also.

Psalm 94:18 *When I said, My foot slippeth; thy "mercy," O Lord, held me up.*

We must trust in His mercies to sustain us each day.

Psalm 13:5 *But I have trusted in thy "mercy"; my heart shall rejoice in thy salvation.*

We must remember that neither our past nor our future sins, cancel out His mercy towards us. Our God is loving and long suffering.

Psalm 25:7 *Remember not the sins of my youth, nor my transgression: according to thy "mercy" remember thou me for thy goodness sake, O Lord.*

There is absolutely nothing that we can do where the Lord does not extend His great mercy unto us. Many people have taken their lives because they felt that they had disappointed the Lord to the degree that His mercy would not be there for them. We are to never allow Satan to cause us to doubt anything about the Lord; that also includes not doubting His mercy.

Arethea Martin Green

Psalm 77:8-9 *Is his "mercy" clean gone forever? doth his promise fail for evermore? Hath God forgotten to be gracious? hath he in anger shut up his tender "mercies"? Selah*

Psalm 77:14 *Thou art the God that doest wonders: thou hast declared thy strength among the people.*

Thank God for His mercies in our lives, especially when we feel that we truly do not deserve them. What a blessing that we can boldly come before His throne and receive mercy, love and whatever we have need of.

We have the privilege to pray for others when they are spiritually weak and God through us can also impart His great mercy unto them.

Conclusion

Thank you for taking the time to read this devotion. I pray that it has blessed you as much as it has me as I wrote it. We all need reminders of the limitless things that the Lord can do in our lives. I am so glad that from His table we may load up our plate and eat from His best. God's blessing, love and mercy to you and as we all continue to live and walk with Him.

Questions To Ponder:

Which verse on mercy encouraged you the most?

What did that particular verse remind you of?

When was the most recent experience of His mercy in your life?

How would you describe God's mercy in your life?

Finish this sentence please, "No matter what I may encounter in life, I know that I will receive God's _____.

Prayer Request:

Chapter Two

Sometimes We Are Empty

*L**uke 11:5-6 And he said unto them, Which of you shall have a friend, and shall go unto him at midnight, and say unto him, Friend, lend me three loaves; For a friend of mine in his journey is come to me, and I have nothing to set before him?*

Jesus was with His disciples praying and as he ceased one of them asked Him to teach them to pray. Jesus taught them to pray and so much more. He gave a great parable about a friend going to another friend in need. When the friend came, his friend had loaves to give to him. We, just as this friend, are sometimes empty and we have nothing to give physically or spiritually.

So many times in the Bible there were empty people, but God provided for them to give. There have been times when Jesus has sent someone in His stead to be a blessing to someone else, nevertheless it was from Him.

The first miracle in the Bible was the wedding in Cana of Galilee. They ran out of wine, but Jesus showed up and performed a miracle. They had no wine, for they were empty.

John 2:7 Jesus saith unto them, Fill the water pots with water. And they filled them up to the brim.

In one day, Jesus fed 5,000 when the disciples were empty. Jesus took the lunch of a small boy who had five loaves of bread and two fishes.

Jesus fed the crowd because the disciples were empty but there was more than enough left over.

John 6:12 *When they were filled, he said unto his disciples, Gather up the fragments that remain, that nothing be lost.*

- David cried out to the Lord many times because he was empty.
- Moses begged God to use someone else because he felt empty.
- Paul had moments in his life that he needed others help because he felt empty.
- Job's friend could not encourage him because they were simply empty.
- The disciples fished all night they caught nothing, their nets were empty.
- The woman came to the well for water and had her bucket and soul filled, for she was empty.

If these people that were mentioned in the Bible had empty moments in their lives, then we should be encouraged during the times that we are empty. Loved ones and friends may come to us and we have nothing to offer because we are empty.

This is the perfect time to help them attain whatever it is that they need, as we help ourselves. We should never be embarrassed when we are empty. Jesus will provide the words that we need to help and He will also provide what is needed physically and materially for those that we are helping.

Prayer is the first response to being empty, spiritual food is always our main source against emptiness. Our hearts may be heavy but prayer will give us exactly what we need. Being empty can be a blessing because it forces us to rely on our inner source, "The Holy Spirit", the only one that can fill up an empty soul. When Jesus fills us up we are completely full. It is common to become empty as a Christian; however, it is not safe to remain that way.

The devil can easily use this time to tempt us to stay there. If we are empty we cannot help ourselves or anyone else. Here are some things that we can do when we become empty.

- Acknowledge to God that we are empty, although He knows; it will remind us of the steps to take when it occurs again.
- Pray and ask the Lord to fill us up again so that we can continue to pour into others spiritually
- Remember and watch for signs of emptiness, we must fill up before we become completely empty, if possible.
- Be mindful that our emptiness does not become "burnout."

Emptiness only comes from sharing and helping others, that is why it is so important that we stay full of the spirit of God. When we are called upon to pray with and encourage others we can become fatigue. Being sensitive to our needs is as vital as the needs of others. A good prayer partner is great to have when we realize that we are pouring into a number of people.

The Lord will bless us even through our emptiness, but we have to remain in tune with the Holy Spirit and that only happens by consistently praying.

We live in a world where people are hurting and a great number are embarrassed that most are Christians. We pull back because we tend to forget that Jesus can fill us up again. We are vessels for Him so it is expected that we would become empty only to be replenished again

Arethea Martin Green

through Him. We must be watchful we must pour out as often as we are filled up. The Lord will send someone your way soon; don't forget it's normal to become empty.

Proverbs 8:21 *That I may cause those that love me to inherit substance; and I will fill their treasures.*

Romans 15:13 *Now the God of hope fill you with all joy and peace in believing, that ye may abound in hope, through the power of the Holy Ghost.*

Over our lifetime, the Lord has sent many people to fill us during droughts in our lives. I am a witness that He has surely blessed my life through others. It is a blessing to be able to pour into the lives of people that He has placed in our path. It is definitely not to be taken lightly and surely not on our own. Pouring into others will cause us to lose strength physically, mentally and spiritually. God's Word reminds us of this struggle.

Ephesians 6:12 *For we wrestle not against flesh and blood, but against principalities, against powers, against the rulers of the darkness of the world, against spiritual wickedness in high places.*

The devil will try to hinder any Christian that prays and aides others against his worldly trap of depression. He knows the power of prayer and therefore he hates any strongholds broken from lives. Not all Christians become empty, because not all Christians pour into others. It is not to look down on anyone because not all Christians are strong enough to endure such a challenge. The Lord has given spiritual abilities differently to each of His servants and there is a job for each of us to do. Pouring into others is not a gift that is given to everyone and He designed it that way on purpose.

That is why it is very important that we pray often and follow the Lord's leading in our lives. When we pour into people and in return we are overwhelmed, then that is not our calling. We then need to connect that person or persons with another Christian that is gifted in that area. This may be a case that takes lengthy prayer and encouraging time. The Lord does not desire that we are discouraged while trying to encourage others.

A great lesson for us to learn ahead of time is that we all will encounter "Emptiness." The key is to realize if we are capable of filling ourselves spiritually and pouring into others or if we are capable of filling ourselves but passing others on to a more spiritually able Christian?

Remember that pouring into others may require spiritual, physical and mental areas. No matter what, the Lord will refill and replenish all that we need. Serving Him is always a privilege and a joy.

Romans 15:13 Now the God of hope fill you with all joy and peace in believing, that ye may abound in hope, through the power of the Holy Ghost.

We all can be encouraged during times of emptiness, the Lord is our God and He is always available to help us in our times of need. He is the only one that is capable of refilling and restoring our lives. Reply on Him!!!

Conclusion

Thank you for reading this devotion, I pray that you have gotten something new from the word of God. I also pray that if you are pouring into people that you are reminded that the Lord sees all that you do and He shall reward you.

Questions To Ponder:

Has there ever been a time that someone came to you when they were empty?

What were they in need of?

How did you respond?

Did you have to go and borrow like the friend in Luke 11 or did you have what they needed?

How well do you track your emptiness? Do you pour out enough that you ever become empty?

Prayer Request:

Chapter Three

Teachers of Good Things

Titus 2:3 The aged women likewise, that they be in behaviour as becometh holiness, not false accusers, not given to much wine, teachers of good things.

In this scripture we are admonished as women to be role models to the younger women. I am afraid to say that this is not so prevalent in today's world. There is a generation of young ladies that has a *know it all* mentality. There are very few young girls interested in being led to live a godly life, especially not being led by another adult woman. There are also some older women that are not interested in investing time to mentor young ladies; they have their own agendas that they are consumed with.

Normally by the age of three, boys and girls can readily tell you their best friend, even if they name an adult. These are people that they have already begun to idolize and mimic. If it is God's will, that person can remain in their lives for a long time because trust has already begun. As parents we then begin to watch the person that our child often speaks about to make sure that the values that we have are also portrayed within this person.

God gave me a friend at the age of four, Anita Otey. She was the first friend that He allowed me to meet. I was not a secure person as a child and I was afraid of most everything. He placed her in my life and we have remained friends until this day. She was definitely a teacher of good things. I watched her love and give of herself for many years. She has the gift of hospitality without a doubt. When we were in grade school she would bring breakfast each morning to those of us that w e r e on our bus stop. As an adult she still gives freely to so many people around her. I am grateful for our friendship. If it were not for the Lord, I would not have such a faithful friend that has taught me so much.

We are teaching when we do not realize that we are. **Titus 2:3** said that we are to be "teachers of good things" not tellers. You see to teach is tell and demonstrate as needed, but to tell is just to talk. Not every person learns audibly - they might need hands on every now and then. Webster defines the word 'teacher' as to cause or help someone to learn about a subject matter, by giving a lesson.

There are guidelines for teaching others; one is to know the manual well and to be familiar with what you are teaching. It does not matter the setting when we are the teacher we must be knowledgeable of what we are teaching. Studying the manual is key to being a successful teacher. As we learn we can teach others, this is why having the right character is so important. What is the right character? That which uplifts and glorifies Christ first, if it does not encourage, edify and glorify Him we are not teaching as Christ taught.

On our jobs we may attend classes or workshops that train us on how to perform the job that we are responsible for. As a Christian we must perform that job as if Christ were our boss and that we were training others to perform the same task as we are. Our promotions are from the Lord and not man, it is He that deems it necessary for raises and promotions.

***Psalm 75:6-7** For promotions cometh neither from the east, nor from the west, nor from the south. But God is the judge: he putteth down one, and setteth up another.*

Our manual is the Word of God, how well do we know the Author of this Great Book? If I were teaching a cooking class and none of the recipes turned out well, no one would be impressed with a class that I chose to teach. I probably would not have anyone to ever sign up again, but if I were to teach your four-year-old and they came home excited and sharing all that they had learned I might become popular and looked upon as a successful teacher. The reason would be that I am far more capable of teaching a preschooler than I am a cooking class, because I am familiar with the manual.

Teaching will always be a part of our society, no matter whether it is positive or negative learning. Teaching and mentoring others comes with a high reward from the Lord. One in which we all will one day give an account of before the Lord. When we teach, what should we be teaching other Christians that may not know?

Teach them **John 3:16** *For God so loved the world, that he gave his only begotten Son, that whosoever believeth in him should not perish,* (go to hell) *but have everlasting life.*

Teach them that outside of Him there is no other way to heaven.

John 3:3 *Jesus answered and said unto him, Verily, verily, I say unto thee, Except a man be born again, he cannot see the kingdom of God.*

John 10:9 *I am the door: by me if any man enter in, he shall be saved, and shall go in and out, and find pasture.*

Teach them that there is no work that we do that can save us, it's only by faith.

Ephesian 2:8-9 *For by grace are ye saved through faith; and that not of yourselves: it is the gift of God. Not of works, lest any man should boast.*

Teach them that because He gave us an everlasting gift we by nature work and serve Him as our thank you, knowing that there are not ever enough works to pay for our sins.

Teach them that when Jesus saves us we have eternal life.

John 10:28-30 *And I give unto them eternal life; and they shall never perish, neither shall any man pluck them out of my hand. My Father, which gave them me, is greater than all; and no man is able to pluck them out of my Father's hand. I and my Father are one.*

Teach them that we all have sinned and we will always sin even after salvation.

Romans 3:23 *For all have sinned, and come short of the glory of God;*

Teach them to ask God to forgive all of their sins each day.

1 John 1:9 *If we confess our sins, he is faithful and just to forgive us our sins, and to cleanse us from all unrighteousness.*

Teach them that we are an example to others; therefore we should display Christ in our lives.

Titus 2:7-8 *In all things shewing thyself a pattern of good works: in doctrine shewing uncorruptness, gravity, sincerity, Sound speech, that cannot be condemned; that he that is of the contrary part may be ashamed, having no evil thing to say of you.*

Teach them that our mannerism speaks volume in our home, church and workplace. We are Christians no matter where we are and our boss and coworkers are watching us.

Titus 2:9-12 *Exhort servants to be obedient unto their own masters, and to please them well in all things; not answering again; Not purloining, but shewing all good fidelity; that they may adorn the doctrine of God our Saviour in all things. For the grace of God that bringeth salvation hath appeared to all men, Teaching us that denying ungodliness and worldly lust, we should live soberly, righteously, and godly, in this present world;*

Teach them why we teach Christ to them.

Titus 2:13-14 *Looking for that blessed hope, and the glorious appearing of the great God and our Saviour Jesus Christ; Who gave himself for us, that he might redeem us from all iniquity, and purify unto himself a peculiar people, zealous of good works.*

Lastly teach them that we are all the same and we have all sinned and still sin, but Jesus died that we might become saved. Until He calls us home we shall never become perfect.

Titus 3:3-6 *For we ourselves also were sometimes foolish, disobedient, deceived, serving divers lust and pleasures, living in malice and envy, hateful, and hating one another. But after that the kindness and love of God our Saviour toward man appeared, Not by works of righteousness which we have done, but according to his mercy he saved us, by the washing of the regeneration, and renewing of the Holy Ghost. Which he shed on us abundantly through Jesus Christ our Saviour;*

These verses sum up the life of all teachers. We can teach with a greater impact if we are transparent to some degree. Our goal should be to reach the heart and need of every student that we teach. Being real is always a help and not presenting a *holier than thou* personality will always capture the attention of the listener.

Conclusion

I thank God that He is the "Master Teacher" that administers tests to us and most times unannounced, but in His grading scale we may always retest if we fail and test as often as needed. This was an intense devotion that may have reminded us that we are all teachers; this manual can never be mastered by man. The Lord does not expect it to be; just reread often. God bless you if you made it to the end of this. I was so deeply moved each time that I worked on it. I only have one question to ask now.

Questions To Ponder

We all have students watching. What type of teacher are you?

Tell God right here what teaching tools that you have need of.

Prayer Request:

Chapter Four

What Does God Say About Children?

P*salm 127:3 Lo, children are a heritage of the Lord: and the fruit of the womb is his reward.*

If you are a woman and gave birth to a child you already know that the pain is worth the joy of seeing that baby for the first time. Parents that adopt children also experience that same feeling on the day that they finally get to bring the child home. A preacher once said, "Having a child is a blessing from God, even when that child may have been considered a surprise baby, but to be adopted is just as much a blessing because that means that the child was chosen (handpicked) to be adopted."

As Christians we were adopted, we were reborn unto God and He adopted us into His family.

Ephesians 1:5-6 Having predestinated us unto the adoption of children by Jesus Christ to himself, according to the good pleasure of his will, To the praise of the glory of his grace, wherein he hath made us accepted in the beloved.

Our biological children sometime resemble either the mother or the father on the inside or out. DNA is the word that man has given, but the Lord calls it right "Created." He created each of us the perfect way that He chose. Our children can take on the resemblance of a parent or that of another family member. It is strange that a child can be born and looks more like an aunt or an uncle than their parents. Unlike our Heavenly Father, we all resemble Him in some way if we are truly His. The devil's children look as he does and so does the Lord's children. Children have always been precious to the Lord. He has so much to say about them in His word. He has given special instructions as how to love and respond to them. He included them all throughout the Bible because He wants us to include them throughout our lives. The word 'children' occurs in 1524 verses of the Bible. Here are a few things that God says about them:

Jesus said that they are the greatest in the kingdom of heaven.

Matthew 18:1-6 *At the same time came the disciples unto Jesus saying, Who is the greatest in the kingdom of heaven? And Jesus called a little child unto him, and set him in the midst of them, And said, Verily I say unto you, Except ye be converted, and become as little children, ye shall not enter into the kingdom of heaven. Whosoever therefore shall humble himself as this little child, in my name receiveth me. But whosoever shall offend one of these little ones which believe in me, it were better for him that a millstone were hanged about his neck, and that he were drowned in the depth of the sea.*

The Bible is the final authority for loving and rearing children. I believe that it is the parents right through Christ as to the way in which they are led to discipline their child/children. We are only accountable to God for our own children and we are not to judge the parenting skills of others.

Jesus said that He wanted children to come unto Him.

Matthew 19:13-15 *Then were there brought unto him little children, that he should put his hands on them, and pray: and the disciples rebuked them. But Jesus said, Suffer little children, and forbid them not, to come unto me: for of* *such is the kingdom of heaven. And he laid his hands on them, and departed thence.*

This verse lets us know that there is a penalty for abusing any child. Those that do will one day answer to the Lord for it. Jesus was born as a baby and He grew up just as we did and our children. I am sure that this was our example that He left us so that we could understand His love for children.

Luke 2:40 And the child grew, and waxed strong in spirit, filled with wisdom: and the grace of God was upon him.

Luke 2:52 And Jesus increased in wisdom and stature, and favour with God and man.

Jesus said that we are to train children.

Proverbs 22:6 Train up a child in the way he should go: and when he is old, he will not depart from it.

Jesus said that children know when they are doing wrong.

Proverbs 20:11 Even a child is known by his doings, whether his work be pure, and whether it be right.

Jesus said that children are to obey their parents, but parents are not to provoke them.

Colossians 3:20-21 Children, obey your parents in all things: for this is well pleasing unto the Lord. Fathers, provoke not your children to anger, lest they be discouraged.

Jesus said that mothers are to keep house and be joyful.

Psalm 113:9 He maketh the barren woman to keep house, and to be a joyful mother of children. Praise ye the LORD.

Being a mother is a joyful time no matter how many children we may have. Although some women suffer before and after pregnancy the joy is still there for them at some point. Mothers that work and being a single surely have a challenge, but there is no love greater than the love of a mother.

Jesus said that children should obey their parents.

Ephesians 6:1 *Children, obey your parents in the Lord: for this is right.*

Proverbs 4:1-2 *Hear, ye children, the instruction of a father and attend to know understanding. For I give you good doctrine, forsake ye not my law.*

Jesus said that children that listen are blessed of Him.

Proverbs 8:32-33 *Now therefore hearken unto me, O ye children: for blessed are they that keep my ways. Hear instruction, and be wise, and refuse it not.*

Jesus said that all children will do foolish things, yet we are to love them.

Proverbs 22:15 *Foolishness is bound in the heart of a child, but the rod of correction shall drive it far from him.*

Jesus said that children need correction.

Proverbs 23:13 *Withhold not correction from the child: for if thou beatest him with the rod, he shall not die.*

Jesus said that the rod of correction along with reproof brings wisdom.

Proverbs 29:15 *The rod and reproof give wisdom: but a child left to himself bringeth his mother shame.*

God warns children of following friends that are disobedient to their parents and others.

Proverbs1:8 *My son, hear the instruction of thy father, and forsake not the law of thy mother:*

Proverbs 1:11 *If they say, Come with us, let us lay wait for blood, let us lurk privily for the innocent without cause:*

Today's children are different from the generation of their parents. It can be very hard at times to convince children that as old as the Bible is, it is still the final judgement for our lives. The Lord still mandates that we teach our children by example first as we give them the words of the Bible. Praying with and for our children is still the order of the day and we cannot allow the difficulty of parenting to stop us from that. In the end when that child does not obey us and develops a rebellious spirit all that we can constantly do is remain in prayer and read them this verse over and over again.

2Timothy 3:15 *And that from a child thou hast known the holy scriptures, which are able to make thee wise unto salvation through faith which is in Christ Jesus.*

It is never wise as a parent to tell or assume that our children are born again, or saved. We should allow them to answer that question for us. True salvation has to be confessed by the mouth of the believer, even when it is our child. Children are pleasers and will tend to agree to whatever their parents assume if it is positive. Heaven is far too precious and eternal for us to assume for them. It is not something that we should feel uncomfortable talking to with them, but if it is you should have a pastor, church worker, or loved one to speak with them. We all only have one life and once God calls us home it's eternal.

Conclusion

Godbless you if you have children or "grand" children. It seems so much easier to love on our grandchildren than our own, yet they are all very important to God. The life and example that we are to them is vital, the one thing that we cannot purchase for them is eternal life with Christ and we do not have to because it is a free gift to all. Lead them, tell them, and teach them of Him and His saving grace. Thank you for reading this devotion and I pray that we reach children for Him.

Questions to Ponder:

What was one childhood memory that you cherish?

Did you receive a Bible as a child?

What was the first scripture that you read that you remember?

What are your views about children (not your own children)?

When do you get the chance to minister to a child?

Prayer Request:

Chapter Five

Good Friendships and Out of Date Calendars

*P**roverbs 18:24 A man that hath friends must shew himself friendly: and there is a friend that sticketh closer than a brother.*

Vicki, Connie and I shared a very close friendship for many years. We gathered once a week with friends at Connie's house to play Bunko for Baskets for three years.

It was a special time to be amongst friends to laugh, eat and catch up on girl talk. Connie was an excellent cook and always planned a special something that all the ladies enjoyed.

Wednesday night Bible Study was always more meaningful because we not only grew spiritually but closer as friends as well. All church events became an extra blessing because our friendship summoned other ladies and their families to join us.

We all made a big deal overall and made sure that no one family received more attention than another. Soon another sweet Vicky and Michael were added to our group and we all grew closer and closer day by day.

I am a firm believer that a close godly friendship can last many years when gossip is omitted and God is glorified. The Lord has allowed the technology of Facebook to keep many of us connected. As our friendships shifted, because we were all military families things were different. God sent three Kim's and their husbands to our group. We eventually had to rotate Bible Studies at Connie's and two of the Kim's home. The Lord sure did give us a number of years to serve together at church and on Friday nights, we were truly "One Big" blended family.

Just as the military does, it separated us over time, but not our love and memories. It is great now to see most of the children then, become successful adults. We have treasured friendships and lasting prayer request that we continue to share.

Only God could have formed such a group as He did and we are all grateful for His blessings upon us. Before we knew it, it was only I, one Kim and two Vicky/Vicki's left and our spouses. Things remained close within us because Jesus was our common bond.

Then one day the Lord sent Sheri, her dad, mom and Tina. It was another round of crazy and having fun in the Lord. Bible Study at the Sherrill's grew and lasted 5 years none stop. Those new groups of children are now all grown up and some are even married.

Friendships through Christ are special and to be treasured, in my opinion. This brings me to the "Out of Date Calendar" portion of this devotion.

Our sweet Connie had moved several years by now, but her silliness she left with us. Sheri was now the new silly of the group. The verse that allows me to describe Vicki is **Psalm 113:9** *He maketh the barren woman to keep house, and to be a joyful mother of children. Praise ye the Lord.*

Vicki Dye is a godly wife, mother and friend. She has mentored and ministered to many women over the years. I am grateful to the Lord for allowing us to serve Him together. Our group became smaller but we often met to have "Hot Wing Gatherings" and we were often the last, loud crew to leave the eatery. One day at Vicki's home she was super excited to tell us of "what she thought was a good online deal." She has recently purchased a leather-bound calendar, the excitement displayed was so Vicki, and it does not take much to make her grateful. She rushed upstairs to get the new calendar that she had waited days to show us.

It was hard for me to be the bearer of "Bad News". I found it quite unusual that she had "Not" realized that the new purchase was nice, but it was an "Out of Date Calendar". It was the year 2015 and the calendar was for 2014!!!! Anna's mom had done it once again!!!! We are all still laughing at that one.

Out of the all the many years of memories as a friend, and there are many. I thank the Lord for allowing the 26 years of our residing in North Carolina to be life changing ones and the blessing is that we will carry these memories to heaven. Your friendship memories may not be an "Out of Date Calendar" one but what are your sweet memories from your friends?

Lastly what a blessing the Lord allowed when He sent Sheri's mom from calm (California) to crazy. God has a sense of humor!

Proverbs 17:17(a) *A friend loveth at all times...*

Conclusion

Let them know how grateful you are and thank you for reading this devotion. May God forever be your comfort!

Arethea Martin Green

Questions to Ponder:

There are no Questions to Ponder, I am sure that we all have a friend/ friends that have impacted our lives, that have prayed us through some tough times in our lives.

Prayer Request:

Chapter Six

The "To Do" List

Colossians 3:23-24 *And whatsoever ye do, do it heartily, as to the Lord, and not unto men. Knowing that of the Lord ye shall receive the reward of the inheritance: for ye serve the Lord Christ.*

In today's society we very often are making a "To Do List." Sometimes we manage to follow it and sometimes we fail. We often make them for our spouse, and children and they do the same for us.

Unless you are an organized person following a list can be very hard to keep up with. Men seem to enjoy using them to make sure that everything is done that is expected of them. Children tend to not like seeing a list, but they know that if they want a certain thing they need to have the list completely checked off.

What if we had to prepare a spiritual "To Do List" what are some things that you would record as a must need each day? Here are a few things that I would compile on mine.

The first thing would be "Listen" **Hebrews 3:7-8** *Wherefore (as the Holy Ghost saith, To day if ye will hear his voice, Harden not your hearts, as in the provocation, in the day of temptation in the wilderness:*

The Israelites did not listen to God while going through the wilderness; therefore many of them did not enter into His rest because of disobedience. God still warns us today not to harden our hearts when the Holy Spirits speaks to us.

Hebrews 3:9-11 *When your fathers tempted me, proved me, and saw my works forty years. Wherefore I was grieved with that generation, and said, They do always err in their heart; and they have not known my ways. So I swear in my wrath, They shall not enter into my rest.)*

Hebrews 3:12 *Take heed, brethren, lest there be in any of you an evil heart of unbelief, in departing from the living God.*

It's difficult to always hear the voice of the Lord silently through our prayers. There are times when the Lord uses others to confirm a direction in which He wants us to take. Not always does it happen that way, God wants our undivided attention often, and so we must wait on Him.

He always answers us, and He is never too late. Listening may mean patience, but it is so worth it in the end.

Hebrews 3:13 *But exhort one another daily, while it is called To day; lest any of you be hardened through the deceitfulness of sin.*

This is the second on the list, "Exhortation" it is still a great need to be practiced today. I believe that we can not only harden our heart towards salvation, but also against things that may cause our walk with the Lord to be hindered. Just as the children of Israel were preached to; so have we that attend church, they did not listen therefore we may be deceived to do the same.

Paying attention during church, bible study and as we read through spiritual material is very important. It is the key to answered prayers and growing more in our spiritual gifts. Asking the Lord to lead you to a loved one or a person that could use a friend or new prayer partner is very rewarding.

Hebrews 4:2 *For unto us was the gospel preached, as well as unto them: but the word preached did not profit them, not being mixed with faith in them that heard it.*

As we exhort others we are also encouraging ourselves. There are hurting hearts all around us, we never know the impact that we can make by simply exhorting one another.

The third thing on the list is "Pray"

When planning, we always should pray, then plan. Developing a habit of asking God first is a form of reverence to Him and His will for us is far above our desires.

James 4:13-15 *Go to now, ye that say, To day or tomorrow we will go into such a city, and continue there a year, and buy and sell, and get gain: Whereas ye know not what shall be on the morrow. For what is your life? It is even a vapour, that appeareth for a little time, and then vanisheth away. For that ye ought to say, If the Lord will, we shall live, and do this, or that.*

We are guilty of it although it is not a good habit to form. We plan our todays and tomorrows as if we are in control and not the Lord. He has blessed us entirely, He allows us to do so much without inviting or asking His blessings upon them. He died so that we could enjoy life and to remember that it is just as James said but a vapour, we can be here today and gone the next second.

Our prayers are our words of burden to the Lord, He longs for us to come to Him as often as we want. There is not a prayer rule or guideline to follow; only sharing what is on our heart that He already knows is there. God does not set a time limit on our prayers He awaits every second of our voice calling out to Him.

Praying is soothing to the soul and when we pray believing, the burdens seem to lift right off. Having a quiet place to pray can definitely relax us and prepare our minds to unload on the God of all comfort.

The fourth and last thing on the list is "Sing"

1Chronicles 16:23 *Sing unto the Lord, all the earth; shew forth from day to day his salvation.*

Psalm 7:17 *I will praise the Lord according to his righteousness: and will sing praises to the name of the Lord most high.*

Psalm 9:2 *I will be glad and rejoice in thee: I will sing praise to thy name, O thou most High.*

Psalm 13:6 *I will sing unto the Lord, because he hath dealt bountifully with me.*

Whether we are in church, home, car etc.... it is good to have a song of praise unto the Lord. David played as unto the Lord. Yes, God does want our prayers and praises but He loves to hear our voices lifted up to Him. Singing and listening to music can be the most rewarding and soothing to the soul. The Lord is not concerned with the way that we sound; He gave us the voice that we have even if we do not feel that it's the best.

Every song has a story and many of them tell of our present issues. We each have a different style of music that we prefer and there is an artist that sings your choice of music. As long as it gives the right opinion of who God is, it will glorify Him as we sing unto Him.

Sometimes we can go through something that is so deep and intense that we need a new song to sing. The scripture speaks of such.

Psalm 40:3 *And he hath put a new song in my mouth, even praise unto our God: many shall see it, and fear, and shall trust in the LORD.*

Psalm 96:1 *O sing unto the LORD a new song: sing unto the LORD, all the earth.*

During a storm in our life we may spend some sleepless nights; that is when we need a song.

Psalm 77:6 *I call to remembrance my song in the night: I commune with mine own heart: and my spirit made diligent search.*

We may experience some weak days and become so burdened and cannot find the right words to pray, that's when we need a song.

Psalm 118:14 *The LORD is my strength and song, and is become my salvation.*

We all can sing because we are thankful to Him for all that He has done for us over and over again, we are to be thankful praisers.

Psalm 69:30 *I will praise the name of God with a song, and will magnify him with thanksgiving.*

This is just the beginning of a list of spiritual things to do each day; of course your list will not be the same as mine because we are thankful for different blessings. Our song may not be the same as well, but we are singing because He deserves our praise through song.

Arethea Martin Green

There are times when I am in my car and I blare my favorite songs and sing and clap as hard and as loud as I can. Our God is worthy of hearing us sing no matter where we are, He delights in hearing the voices that He created.

Conclusion

I pray that you have enjoyed this "Spiritual to Do List" I also pray that whomever you are that the Lord will be all that you trust and believe Him to be in your life. God bless you and all those that are dear to you, thanks again and may He be first on your list of things "To Do". We were surely on His.

Questions to Ponder

Are you a list maker?

Why do you feel it necessary or unnecessary to make a list?

Where is God on the list of things "to do" in your life?

When you pen a list for yourself or others, do you leave a sweet word or verse at the end?

Following a list can help us become more sensitive to the needs of others. Just as we do not always finish what do we will think of them when they don't?

What do you think?

Prayer Request:

Chapter Seven

America, Our Veterans Need Us!

Romans 10:1 *Brethren, my heart's desire and prayer to God for Israel (America) is, that they might be saved.*

Paul had a burden for the people of Israel to become saved. My heart has the same prayer for America. We need more Christians for the times in which we live; Christians that will take a spiritual stand.

What happened to America? This is a very broad question to ask, yet I am sure that many wonder the same. There are numerous answers to this question and we all have our own opinions as to what we view as the problem. We as a nation have committed many mistakes over the years; some that we can recover from and others that we cannot.

There are three immediate things that I view about America that has caused a drastic change. The first is that the Lord Jesus Christ is not welcomed in a nation that He created. Yes, the Holy Spirit is present among the "Believers" but the God of this universe is not welcomed completely.

Jesus is knocking at the hearts and homes of America, waiting to be invited in to save and minister to souls.

Revelations 3:20 *Behold, I stand at the door, and knock: if any man hear my voice, and open the door, I will come in to him, and will sup with him, and he with me.*

Secondly, "Sin" is a joke to a great number of people in

our nation. Any race or gender is allowed to commit whatever crime they desire and are given years before trial dates or convictions are made. Often times the person would have added more crimes before the first crime is dealt with. This causes a cycle from one generation to another, because nothing happens in a timely manner.

Ecclesiastes 8:11 *Because sentence against "evil work" is not executed speedily, therefore the heart of the sons of men is fully set in them to do evil.*

This is the prime reason the devil can convince crime in the minds of those that have no hope.

Thirdly, the "crown of pride" has fallen from our heads as a nation. Lady Liberty stands with a crown on her head because we were once a proud nation that stood tall. We offered constant pride and love, we were a community that embraced and prayed as "One." July 4th was the most decorated and festive where flags were displayed on every street corner.

Lamentations 5:16 *The crown is fallen from our head: woe unto us, that we have sinned.*

We have allowed Republican and Democratic Party beliefs to cause us to disrespect those in office and our fellowman. We seem to have forgotten that no matter who is elected president, "Jesus is King" of this nation. There is a verse that covers the position of both our pastors and president that we are to remember and obey.

Hebrews 13:17 *Obey them that have the rule over you, and submit yourselves: for they watch for your souls, as they that must give account, that they may do it with joy, and not with grief: for that is unprofitable for you.*

Pastors and presidents (along with those that serve under them) are to be prayed for as they serve us, under the leadership of the Lord. The Lord does not require prayers for them if they met our guidelines, we are just to trust Him and pray for them.

These were just three immediate things that trouble me about America, although I know that we all have our own opinions. I must say that among all of its down falls America is still "The Best" nation to be a part of. I am proud to be an American and believe that God blesses and loves us all!!!

I must close with sharing my heart about a strong group of people that has given so much to America. Our military!!!!!! These men and women surely deserve more than they are given. It would be my desire to see everyone visit a Veterans Hospital, which is one of the most heart touching places to visit along with St. Jude Hospital, all Children's Hospitals and Nursing Homes are precious places that need our prayers daily.

Veterans!!!! Deserve our highest regards from our nation; they are treated as second class from a nation that they have served "First Class."

A few months ago I walked into a Veterans Hospital for the first time in my life; I was definitely not prepared for what I experienced. The tears would not cease from flowing, I received the shock of my life. This was just from the clinic side, not the main hospital. All races, genders and branches were present; they were doing as they were taught protecting and defending each other's needs. They preferred to defend one another, even though they were just as needy as the other. I tell you, it was a blessing to witness so much love among them from day to day.

One day as I sat there I thought to myself. What if when men and women were getting ready to take the "Oath" if they were shown a potential before and after picture, how many would "Swear In" The after you serve pictures are the results of what we see in the Veterans Hospitals: homeless Veterans, missing limbs, PTSD, body braces, disfigured faces and so much more including dentures, scratches and cuts, missing toes and fingers and again the list goes on. They served for us and many would do it again and again, some would still take the "Oath" if they could view a potential after you've served picture.

"All have given a service, but some have given even their lives." Their loved ones had to go on and grow on without them; oh I totally understand that they are aware of this when they accept the call to duty. That does not change the fact that in America the ones with the earthly power to do better for those that have served will not. Not because I have a dad, husband and two sons that serve and have served, but because my heart hurts that the land that they once defended, seem to have "Forgotten."

Every day is Veterans Day now to me, I have been deeply moved by the picture that is etched in my mind each time I visit there. Not a day goes by that I am not stirred to tears and prayer. At first I did not think that I could endure the visits, but I had no choice. It became a new prayer and appreciation to me; I was afforded an opportunity to pray for veterans and their families.

Join me as we remind them that not <u>Just</u> in November, but each day we love and appreciate all that they have done. America is a "Great Nation" but, it can become "The

Greatest Nation" when we begin to "Serve Those That Deserve" and that would be our "Hero's the Veterans".

Join me!!! Let's pray together that the "White House," the president and congress will all be burdened to give greater attention to the needs of our veterans and their loved ones. Prayer changes things and it can begin with us!!!! Find a veteran and ask them to share a fun story of their military experience.

"In God We Trust" cannot continue to be written on our currency and not on our hearts. A vital part of trusting Him would be through rewarding our Victorious Veterans.

Conclusion

Thank you for reading this devotion; it was one that I became very passionate about as I was writing it. I was not expecting God to use this experience as one to share; nevertheless it's just like Him to surprise us!!

God bless you and any of your loved ones or friends that have served our great country. Together we can all do better, especially through prayer.

Questions to Ponder:

What makes America great to you?

Do you know of any veterans?

List just a few of their names, and then pray for them now, please.

Would you be willing to ask a veteran to share their story with you?

Are there times that you display an American Flag, whether large or small, if no, not why not?

Prayer Request:

Chapter Eight

Arguing for Nothing

Job 6:25 How forcible are right words! but what doth your arguing reprove?

Have you ever had an argument with someone? You had a concrete reason, but you simply got nowhere? We all can probably attest to this happening at some time in our lives. Some people thrive on confrontation; they look for any reason or anything that causes conflict.

Job's friends were trying to cause a conflict with him. They wanted him to admit that he was the reason for all that he was going through. Job stood his ground; he had too much going on to argue with them. There may have been times when we talked to the person, or tried to talk. We may not have gotten a word in because the person controlled the entire conversation. Nevertheless, when it is all said and done, it is not rare to realize that sometimes we may have been arguing for "Nothing".

Job said it perfectly for us how forcible are right words. We can be saying everything that is correct and yet walk away unheard. Satan enjoys it when people argue and as a matter of fact, he wants it to happen often. I am quite sure that he glories more when families and close friends are at odds with one another. Chances are when its family or close friends the hurt is deeper. Harsh words may be used and old unresolved conflicts feaster. Someone could very well bring up resentment or bitter areas that they never revealed before.

Unresolved arguments can cause bitterness and if it is a

sensitive subject, things may never change. It is impossible to go through life and not have an argument or disagreement with someone. It is not impossible to learn from the first to avoid a second. If we walked away hurt or feeling unanswered, we have experienced some of the effects from it. Arguments arise from offenses and as humans we shall at some time offend.

James 3:2 *For in many things we offend all. If any man offend not in word, the same is a perfect man, and able also to bridle the whole body.*

Having the last words as Christians is not important at all. Walking away before the argument begins displays the spiritually strong person. Yes, we can choose to remain and verbally destroy our testimonies and talk back and forth but what will it prove? The person that walks away has a more positive view of life and foresees the ruin that arguing may cause.

Choosing to leave the situation does not indicate that we are not offended; we have only traded peace over revenge. The Christian journey is all about enduring and becoming a stronger soldier of Christ daily. We learn to love God and His word more and it becomes a shield for our hearts. We develop a resistance to things that are ungodly, because we know that He will take good care of us.

Psalm 119:165 *Great peace have they which love thy law: and nothing shall offend them.*

We all can agree that it is hard to walk away when harsh words are being used towards us. This verse should help us to brace our emotions when adversity comes. The world views a person as a coward if they do not defend themselves, but the Bible states it totally differently.

Job 6:30 *Is there iniquity in my tongue? cannot my taste discern perverse things?*

Job 27:4 *My lips shall not speak wickedness, nor my tongue utter deceit.*

Job knew the power of hateful words; he knew that it would only cause an argument for nothing!! Only the devil wins after every encounter, both or all participants leave with a wounded spirit. Hateful words can ruin the sender and the receiver, often we do not seem to care at the moment. The tongue speaks both life and death and it is a powerful tool.

Proverbs 18:21 *Death and life are in the power of tongue: and they that love it shall eat the fruit thereof.*

Psalm 52:2 *The tongue deviseth mischief; like a sharp razor, working deceitfully.*

James 3:8 *But the tongue can no man tame; it is an unruly evil, full of deadly poison.*

The devil is the author of confusion, he uses arguments to divide families and friends every chance that he can. One simple argument can cause many to part ways and no longer love or fellowship again. Anger causes unresolved conflict and if not dealt with it later becomes bitterness. When bitterness is planted it grows thick and prickly as a cactus and not many can stand to be around it. We are born for adversity, but not taught to entertain it.

Proverbs 17:17 *A friend loveth at all times, and a brother is born for adversity.*

Ephesians 4:26 *Be ye angry, and sin not: let not the sun go down upon your wrath:*

Romans 12:18 *If it be possible, as much as lieth in you, live peaceably with all men.*

This is when the silent tongue and walking away takes place, Job said it best.

Job 14:1 *Man that is born of woman is of few days and full of troubles.*

One of our troubles of life may be those "Forcible Words." Be ready; pray right away, do your best to respond as a strong Christian, God is already there acknowledge His presence.

Conclusion

Thank you for reading this devotion, I pray that it can help you or someone that you know. Not all confrontations are workable and sometimes people and situations are better left unsaid and undone. The Lord will lead us to what is best. Always remember "Forgive even when we can't Forget, God bless your day!

Questions To Ponder:

When was your last argument?

How did you respond? Were there harsh words expressed?

Where do you stand now with that person?

Did you quickly catch yourself and smooth it over, or do you need to stop and pray and ask God now to help you?

Prayer Request:

Chapter Nine

Things We Say When We Are Hurting

*P**salm 109: 1-2 Hold not thy peace, O God of my praise; For the mouth of the wicked and the mouth of the deceitful are open against me: they have spoken against me with a lying tongue.*

David was wounded from the mouths of others, his heart was hurting and his spirit was down. He prayed a prayer unto the Lord for help during his time of deep despair. In this chapter we may all find ourselves during some dark times of hurt in our own lives.

We are no different than David or anyone else in the Bible, we have and will experience some not so pleasant days in life. Although he sinned with Bathsheba, God forgave him and used his life to encourage ours. Experiencing hatred from a loved one or friend can be difficult to deal with. We may not always know the words nor the spiritual way to respond.

A human response might come to us before a spiritual one, when our spirit is wounded. I am so comforted and joyful that no matter what we may endure; the Lord has already gone before us and provided the proper response. Although we may react in the flesh first there is still a spiritual recovery along with His forgiveness. It may cost us some recovery time or we may lose that relationship that is why we are to react through prayer before using our mouths.

David had some strong feelings that he shared that we all

are familiar with. It is interesting that there are those that demand apologies, yet they refuse to ask forgiveness from others. David appears to be fed up with mankind. Many times I have read this chapter and saw myself and had to laugh. God does have a sense of humor and he does allow us to openly express ourselves. We feel as though we can tell the Lord how to handle our issues, knowing that He does not need our help.

I am sure that there has been times when He laughed at my ideas of what I thought were best for me. He created us and He knows what is most profitable for us, yet He laughs and continues to love us.

Psalm 126:2 *Then was our mouth filled with laughter, and our tongue with singing: then said they among the heathen, The Lord hath done great things for them.*

God desires that we find joy even during our trails, for He has not forgotten us.

Proverbs 17:22 *A merry heart doeth good like a medicine: but a broken spirit drieth the bones.*

It does not take much to be joyful, seeing another day should give us a joyful heart. David is a prime example of words that we say when we are hurting. Let's look at somethings that he shared from his hurting, broken spirit.

David was God's man and God allowed him to display his human side so that we could be encouraged. Find yourself in **Psalm 109**; our God has definitely left us a book of instructions that are His blueprints for our lives.

I love the fact that David started out with praise in verse 1, **Psalm 109:1** *"Hold not thy peace, O God of my praise."* then he began to share his hurting heart. The Lord hears us even during our anger; He understands all that we encounter.

David said that they fought him without cause and they awarded him evil for good, yet he prayed.

Psalm 109:3-5 *They compassed me about also with words of hatred; and fought against me without cause. For my love they are adversaries: but I give myself unto prayer. And they have rewarded me evil for good, and hatred for my love.*

Psalm 109: 6-7 *"Set thou a wicked man over him: and let Satan stand at his right hand. When we shall be judged, let him be condemned: and let his prayer become sin."*

David was so angry that he wished bad and no mercy for the man's job, wife and children.

Psalm 109:8-10 *"Let his days be few; and let another take his office. Let his children be fatherless, and his wife a widow. Let his children be continually vagabonds,*(moving from place to place without a home) *and beg: let them seek their bread also out of their desolate places."*

Psalm 109:12 *Let there be none to extend mercy towards him: neither let there be any to favour his fatherless children.*

Psalm 109:17 *As he loved cursing, so let it come unto him: as he delighted not in blessing, so let it be far from him.*

David was hurting, but he cried out to the Lord for help. When we are experiencing this type hurt we must do the same.

Psalm 109:20-22 *Let this be the reward of mine adversaries from the Lord, and of them that speak evil against my soul. But do thou for me, O God the Lord, for thy name's sake: because thy mercy is good, deliver thou me. For I am poor and needy, and my heart is wounded within me.*

David summed it up for us of things that we might say when we are hurting. There is more there I did not quote so that you could go and finish the chapter. It is a comfort to read this so that we can see that we are all human and also to see what anger can cause.

Job's wife also had a moment of anger and harsh words. She was tired of seeing her husband go through so much; that it caused her to speak wrongly.

Job 2:9 *Then said his wife unto him, Dost thou still retain thine integrity? curse God and die.*

Job 2:10*, But he said unto her, Thou speaketh as one of the foolish women speaketh. What? shall we receive good at the hand of God, and shall we not receive evil? In all this did not Job sin with his lips.*

What a good chapter to reflect upon when our hearts are hurting and we are fed up with the mouths of others. Just as David asked for mercy and help we must remember to ask also.

Conclusion

Thank you for reading this devotion, isn't it a blessing to serve a God that is fully concerned with our feelings. What a comfort to serve a God that we can express our thoughts from our hurt. God bless your day and I pray His best for your life as well as mine.

Questions to Ponder:

Did you find yourself in Psalm 109?

Which verses spoke to you the most?

What was the most recent thing that happened that caused you such hurt?

How did you handle it?

What did you learn from Psalm 109 that will help you next time?

Prayer Request:

Chapter Ten

Waiting On Your Next Journey

Isaiah 40:31 *But they that wait upon the Lord shall renew their strength; they shall mount up with wings as eagles; they shall run, and not be weary; and they shall walk, and not faint.*

Out of all the things in life to do "waiting" seems to be one of the hardest. Not long ago a friend (Carrie Davies) and I were both heading into a new journey in our lives. A new chapter was not the appropriate word because in my mind chapters in life simply mean the same routine, but at a different place or pace. A journey would indicate bigger things are happening; a new location and totally entering into a huge unknown. Seemingly more as a new faith walk, trusting God for the unknown, while He has confirmed that this is the road to follow.

My friend and I would text each day, sometimes more than once. We relied on the prayers and words of encouragement to carry us through. I remember sharing with her once when we both felt spiritually drained that God had given me a new focus for that day. I shared that just as if we were in a doctor' office we check in and have a seat. After a while our names would be called. That thought has carried me for the past months, Jesus knows that I am there, He sees me waiting and soon He shall give answer to the problem that I have.

Following God's call to move back to Alabama was definitely a new journey. After being away from this city for 35 years it was indeed a leap of faith. A new book was being written in our life and I was not the one writing it.

The comfort that the Lord gave was my friend. We both liked doing new things. It was our crafty personalities that struck such joy within us and caused us to have so much in common. Well, God had a bigger plan for our friendship and neither of us would have figured a new journey would be involved.

Philippians 4:11 *Not that I speak in respect of want: for I have learned, in whatsoever "state" I am, therewith to be content.*

I took this scripture literally. I embraced that now living in the state of Alabama, I needed to be content. I was reminded that we were embarking upon a new journey, that would require carrying enough spiritually to sustain us. This was not an overnight trip that required an overnight bag or one piece of luggage. It was all about being prepared for detours and maybe even a few problems along the way. Maybe we had to be ready and dressed for the adventure and expect some spiritual inclement weather, flat tires, running out of gas and of course some road blocks. We would need to pray and put on the whole of God's armour.

Ephesians 6:11 *Put on the whole armour of God, that ye may be able to stand against the wiles of the devil.*

During a short trip or long journey, we may find ourselves veering away from the "Compass of Life". We may take the wrong exit or miss a road sign. We underestimate the amount of gas (power) that we have in our spiritual tank. We end up off course and run into dead end streets. It becomes necessary to then glance again at the compass and navigator of our lives, He is Jesus. It is best to pull over and pray and ask Him to redirect us. This is so common in the Christian journey. We so often lose sight of His plans for us, we find ourselves lost and side tracked.

We get ahead of the spiritual map that He has given to us, we forget that He knows what is best for us. We want to rely on the road that someone has taken thinking that it will lead us in the same location, but the Lord's ways are not ours nor His plans.

Isaiah 55:8 For my thoughts are not yours thoughts, neither are your ways my ways, saith the Lord.

Jeremiah 29:11 For I know the thoughts that I think towards you saith the Lord, thoughts of peace, and not evil, to give you an expected end.

Journeys, just as quick trips could possibly cause us to wait for a while; patience is a necessity. It's the perfect time to rethink things that are needed for the trip, whether there are others or not being prepared. Pray before leaving. We always want God's protection. Bring some good entertainment to share along the way. Encouraging others and enquiring about their prayer needs and likes always makes a trip more adventurous.

Celebrate the arrival!!!! We can never forget the Lord once we reach our destination. He was the one that carried us there. We have to remember to include God in all of our trips, whether they are quick or extended and when we arrive be excited and praise Him.

1 Thessalonians 5:16 Rejoice evermore.

I have learned so much more about myself and I have also learned to lean on Jesus closer than ever before. My friend and I shared some of our valley experiences along the way, it has been a challenge and a lot of unexpected side roads were traveled getting here. I did learn that it was all inclusive; the purpose to get away was for my friend and I to become closer friends, to rely on God and to realize that it was His plan for our lives. I found the sweetest verse to fit the journeys within my life, next time I will be better prepared because I have learned to follow and trust Him more.

Psalm 90:14 *O satisfy us early with thy mercy; that we may rejoice and be glad all of our days.*

Conclusion

Thank you for taking the time to read this devotion, on purpose the Lord allowed me to write it and I am grateful. I pray that your journeys are not overwhelming and that you remember that when the time comes Jesus is there.

Questions To Ponder:

When was your last journey?

Were you nervous although you knew that the Lord was there?

Was it a smooth transition or were there a few problems?

What scripture or prayer encouraged you along the way?

Did you celebrate and thank Jesus at your arrival, what did you learn?

Prayer Request:

Chapter Eleven

The Virtuous, Nagging Woman

P*roverbs 31:10 Who can find a virtuous woman? for her price is far above rubies.*

Proverbs 27:15 A continual dropping in a very rainy day and a contentious woman are alike.

Both of these scriptures are referenced from the King James Bible. The Lord inspired them because they both go hand in hand. It is so amazing that we may steer away from reading Proverbs 31 because we feel as though we cannot find ourselves there.

May I have the liberty to say that we are all in this Proverbs 31. No, we may not be all verses in **Proverbs 31:10-29**, (no woman is). These are the words of King Lemuel's mother. They are words that she taught her son; qualities that she gave him to seek within a woman. A virtuous woman is hard to find and many women have given up on the role of being a mother. They have allowed others to step in and take over their responsibilities. I challenge us to read **Proverbs 31** more intently and find ourselves and build from it spiritually. This is to include single moms and young ladies; we must remind ourselves of the spiritual worth that we have.

I boldly proclaim **Proverbs 31** verse 12 as my marital verse, *"She will do him good and not evil all the days of her life."* When my husband leaves the toilet seat up in the middle of the night, or his clothes in the middle of the floor constantly, this verse calms my thoughts and I find myself quoting it so many times. If we are going to make it from day to day, we have to develop a sense of humor even to the things of God. He knew that the virtuous woman can also be a nagging woman as well. It does not give us permission to nag, but it does cause us to laugh when we read about us. The Lord warned men of a contentious woman. He created us therefore He knows what we are capable of.

God said that it would be better to sit on top of a roof and we can all relate to the annoying constant dropping of water. When a woman is unhappy, more than likely, some nagging will happen. It is a part of our spiritual DNA. It is a natural response for us, although it does not put the receiver in a happy place.

Proverbs 21:19 *It is better to dwell in the wilderness, than with a contentious and an angry woman.*

Proverbs 27:15 *A continual dropping in a very rainy day and a contentious woman are alike.*

We all know a few women that we would describe as a virtuous woman, these are ladies that we hold with high spiritual regard. These women may fit your idea of **Proverb 31** verses 10-29, yet they can also be naggers when they deem it necessary.

The Lord does not set us up for failure that is why I believe He has allowed us to see the examples of so many lives in the bible. We are to learn more of Him and ourselves as we read the Holy Bible. It is a spiritual mirror for us that we are to look into and make the necessary changes.

I had never looked at Proverbs 31 in this light until the day that the Lord gave me this devotion to write. It was written to encourage myself and others to recognize ourselves more in Proverbs 31 and to see that the virtuous and nagging woman both exist together. We must also remember that the nagging woman does not nag for eternity. If a woman is a constant nagger to her spouse, children, family or friends; no one will come around. No one wants to be in the company of a "nagger" and it can be a quick turn off to all that has to encounter this nagging on a daily basis and especially in the work place or church. This type of spirit is not Christ-like and we must ask Jesus to remove it from us. **Proverbs 31** verse 26 is a perfect scripture.

Proverbs 31:26 She openeth her mouth with wisdom; and in her tongue is the law of kindness.

What a verse for us to embrace if we desire to end the spirit of nagging.

Psalms 141:3 Set a watch, O Lord, before my mouth; keep the door of my lips.

Conclusion

Thank you for reading this devotion, I trust that you found a sense of humor as you found or reminded yourself in Proverbs 31. God bless your life and may He be your source of joy each day.

Questions to Ponder:

Which verses in Proverbs 31 best describe you?

Which godly woman came to your mind as you read through it?

We all can be a nagger, what puts you in a nagging mode?

Do you think that you can catch yourself now and back away from nagging?

Would you be honest with that person and admit that you are nagging them and ask for forgiveness? How victorious that would be!!!

Prayer Request:

Chapter Twelve

Things That Stink!

Ecclesiastes 10:1 Dead flies cause the ointment of the apothecary to send forth a stinking savour: so doth a little folly him that is in reputation for wisdom and honour.

When we are endeavoring as Christians to live a good, godly life things can happen along the way that cause us to stop and say, "Man That Stinks."

We can cause the stinking smell in our own lives. Getting off track is normal in the Christian walk. One day I was sitting on my sofa reading and the Lord gave me this devotion. As I read what I'd written, I had to laugh to myself as I thought, "What a title!"

We can be so hard on ourselves; we feel as though we are required to be super Christians and we are not. The Lord wants us to accept His free gift of eternal life, make Him Lord of our lives and love Him. As we find our way spiritually, He is there to guide us. He knows that we will struggle with things and He does not expect us to have the answers, but to come to Him because He does.

Romans 3:23 For all have sinned, and come short of the glory of God;

Preachers, teachers, creatures - we all sin and that will never change. We must not enjoy and make sinning a game. The Lord knew that this walk would not be easy, that is why it's called a walk.

John 16:33 *These things I have spoken unto you, that in me ye might have peace. In the world ye shall have tribulation: but be of good cheer; I have overcome the world.*

We are to enjoy reading God's word as we learn more about Him. Everyone retains more when they can enjoy as they learn. There are many scriptures that shows that the Lord has a sense of humor. He wants us to laugh as we learn of His goodness. We all resemble the characteristics of someone in the Bible, we may not have found that person, but it is true.

"Things That Stink", is a simple devotion for the writer and the reader. Jesus gave it to me and it is not intended to point a spiritual finger at anyone, it is a simple devotion with biblical truths for us. No one is holier than another. We are all found in this verse.

1 Timothy 1:15 *This is a faithful saying, and worthy of all acceptation, that Christ Jesus came into the world to save sinners; of whom I am chief.*

This is one verse that resembles us all, but there are more. Keep reading and you will find yourself and it will cause you to smile.

It is always my desire to encourage myself and others through His word; these are a few things that may "Stink" in our lives:

It "stinks" when the person that we marry decides that they no longer desire to remain as one. The Lord hates divorce, yet He permits it, because some circumstances cause us to go our separate ways. If divorce is the only option, leave in peace if possible.

Romans 12:18 *If it be possible, as much as lieth in you, live peaceably with all men.*

Arethea Martin Green

It "stinks" when our children, that we have raised in a Christian home have no desire to live their lives for the Lord. We are not held responsible for the life that our children live once they are out of our home. If we have provided for them and they choose differently, we then can only pray for them and trust the Lord that those prayers will track them down.

Proverbs 22:6 *Train up a child in the way he should go: and when he is old, he will not depart from it.*

Even the rebellious child has a conscience. You may not see the regret of not listening, but it is there hidden and convicting. When parents love and pour into their children for years, the devil is not happy because he wants the souls of children. When we have done all that we can; then all that is left is constant prayers and unconditional love. No matter what your child does love them through it, they need you as the parent. Remember Adam and Eve had the "Best Father," yet even they did not obey and neither did we.

It "stinks" when a family member turns their back on us when we have been there for them. Love through it, live through it and pray through it, do not allow it to consume you. Separation from the person is sometimes needed, just do not allow bitterness to settle, love from a distance and pray for that loved one.

Psalm 41:9 *Yea, mine own familiar friend* (loved one) *in whom I trusted, which did eat of my bread, hath lifted up his heel against me.*

This can be painful, but it happens and if we cannot settle it with the loved one, move on and grow on in Christ.

It "stinks" when friends and neighbors cause us heartache and disappointment, many people are closer to their neighbors and friends than they are to their relatives. When we have friends we must extend the love that we want to receive, unfriendly people may not have many friends or none at all.

Proverbs 17:17 *A friend loveth at all times and a brother is born for adversity.*

Proverbs 18:24 *A man that hath friends must shew himself friendly: and there is a friend that sticketh closer than a brother.*

Although the bible commands us to love our neighbors, neighbors are not as close anymore. If you live in a neighborhood and your neighbors are friendly and look out for each other that is rare. It is always refreshing to see block parties and neighborhood yard sales; those things just do not appear very much.

Matthew 22:39 b.....Thou shalt love thy neighbor as thyself.

It "stinks" when coworkers cannot dwell in unity in the work place. Stress within a person can become higher from our jobs than from our homes. Every person deserves to have a stress-free work environment, mainly because we are there more hours a day than we are at home. Some Christian based business' have little to no unity at all, when it is so vital. Every employee should come to work knowing that it is stress-free; a happy worker is a faithful worker.

Psalm133:1 *Behold, how good and how pleasant it is for brethren to dwell in unity.*

It takes strong leadership in the home, church, workplace and school for things to be ran smoothly and in unity. Prayer has been removed across the board in so many places; therefore, we can only rely on prayer and Christian character to take place.

It "stinks' that America has become so heartless and full of murder, robbery, scammers, haters and liars. So many ungodly things have crept into the church. Teachers are taking sexual advantage of their students and church leaders cannot be trusted around children. There is so much going on in this world.

America has lost its universal cry for peace and freedom. The words printed on our currency is but a lie as a whole. "In God We Trust" remains only in the hearts of a few Americans.

It "stinks" that criminals commit more crimes by the time that they go to court for the first one, therefore they have no desire but to continue to do wrong.

***Ecclesiastes 8:11** Because sentence against an evil work is not executed speedily, therefore the heart of the sons of men is fully set in them to do evil.*

"One Nation Under God" is not noticeable anymore. Prayer is the need for this time and although America is still a great nation, it has surely fallen away from being the Greatest.

The things that "stink" is infinite in our lives. We each have different pet peeves that get under our skin sometimes. Nevertheless, God is still God and He is always in control and He is alive and watching over us eternally. Each day that He allows us to see is another chance to do things different from the day before. Keep praying and believing none of these things have taken the Lord by surprise.

Psalm 121:4 *Behold, he that keepeth Israel* (the world) *shall neither slumber nor sleep.*

Conclusion

Thank you for taking your time to read this devotion; it is my desire that you enjoyed some part of it. I pray that the Lord will be all that you need in your life and that you look for His small blessing as well as the large. God bless your day and again thanks.

Questions to Ponder:

There are no Questions to Ponder.

Prayer Request:

Chapter Thirteen

Living In A Manhole

P*salm 40:2 He brought me up also out of an horrible pit, out of the miry clay, and set my feet upon a rock, and established my goings.*

We do not have to be suffering from depression in order to feel as though we want to just jump into a "manhole". Sometimes life can become very complicated. It is normal to sense that things will not change for the good in our lives. There may be times when we have done all the right things. We have prayed and waited and prayed and waited, yet things do not seem to move or God does not answer our prayers when we want.

When things seem to spiral down and sit there, we may feel compelled to "throw in the towel", on life. This is when we feel that we are in a spiritual manhole. Job was at a point in his life that he may have felt similar to us.

Job 10:1 My soul is weary of my life; I will leave my complaint upon myself; I will speak in the bitterness of my soul.

Here are a few reasons why we may feel as though we are in a spiritual manhole:

1. Manholes are deep and dark. If we cover the hole, no one knows that we are there.

2. Manholes are everywhere within the cities. There is usually one right next to the other. How similar is this to our situations, there is usually a person or two hurting just as we are. We see them, but have no idea that they

are going through a difficult time as well.

3. People pass by manholes daily, but all of the movement can prevent them from knowing someone is there. Such as the busy world today we become so distracted that we tend to not notice things around us. This is when we need to remember *1 Samuel 30:6 c ... but David encouraged himself in the LORD his God.* As hard as it may have been, sometimes we have to hold on to His truths and encourage ourselves in the LORD as David did.

4. Manholes can only be entered for a limited time. When city workers enter them they do not dwell there long, even if they have to return the next day. And eventually their work there is done. We have to do the same when we enter that spiritual manhole of drought. We cannot remain there forever.

Psalm 119:50 This is my comfort in my afflictions: for thy word has quickened me.

A spiritual reconnection is important during this time. *Job 9:27 If I say, I will forget my complaint, I will leave off my heaviness, and comfort myself:* The Lord has provided us with all the proper tools to help us fix all of our problems, if only we but use them.

5. Manholes are frequently checked to ensure that all things are working properly. A technician will come by to render a complete look over, there can be no one left there beyond work time. The Lord Jesus does the same for us. He has appointed Christians to stop by and check on us, He does not leave us alone. Sometimes more than one visit or person is required to help us out of the dark spiritual manhole that we are in.

He made us and He knows all about us. He has great plans for our lives.

Arethea Martin Green

Psalm 139:2 *Thou knowest my downsitting and mine uprising, thou understandest my thought afar off.*

Jeremiah 29:11-13 *For I know the thoughts that I think toward you, saith the LORD, thoughts of peace, and not of evil, to give you an expected end. Then shall ye call upon me, and ye shall go and pray unto me, and I will hearken unto you. And ye shall seek me, and find me, when ye shall search for me with all your heart.*

The lord loves us and He knows that we all will "GROW" through some things as we live for Him.

Why do Christians enter spiritual manholes?

*Because struggle is normal in the Christian life.

*We grow through our trials and tribulations.

*It is normal to feel far away from the Lord, when our prayers are not answered speedily.

*Because we forget that we are human and not super saints.

*Because the Lord loves us, and we cannot be conformed without change.

2Corinthians 1:3-4 *Blessed be God, even the Father of our Lord Jesus Christ, the Father of mercies, and the God of all comfort; Who comforteth us in all our tribulation, that we may be able to comfort them which are in any trouble, by the comfort wherewith we ourselves are comforted of God.*

Sometimes manholes are never left open, but there is always a barrier to warn others of the danger of falling into them. When we experience the darkness of a spiritual manhole we should warn others of the possible outcome. Not all recover from spiritual droughts, we must stand guard and share with others of the way that the Lord pulled us out. Remember the ones that the Lord allowed to pass our way and for some of us He had to send more than one person.

***1Thessalonians 5:14-15** Now we exhort you, brethren, warn them that are unruly, comfort the feebleminded, support the weak, be patient toward all men. See that none render evil for evil unto any man; but ever follow that which is good, both among yourselves, and to all men.*

Conclusion

Thank you for reading this devotion, I pray that the Lord will continue to bless your life and those that are near and dear to you. We all have experienced some dark days in our lives, it may not have been the same situations but the same outcome. Jesus!! He either calls us to Him or through Him he works everything all out, either way we win because He never makes a mistake.

Questions to Ponder:

There are no "Questions To Ponder", just thoughts to remember:

Manholes are not off limits but we can only dwell there for a limited time.

Joseph received great blessings after the "PIT" and so will we.

Again, God bless you, He is all that we need to succeed in this life.

Prayer Request:

Chapter Fourteen

Let's Just Stop Fooling Ourselves

Hebrews 5:12 *For when for the time ye ought to be teachers, ye have need that one teach you again which be the first principles of the oracles of God; and are become such as have need of milk, and not of strong meat.*

A few years ago this scripture hit me pretty hard; it was a tough pill to swallow as true as it was for me. I was not amazed that the Lord laid it on my heart to write about it, seeing that He loves for us to share our experiences. As Christians when we become convicted we are to pray and ask the Lord to lead us in making the necessary adjustments spiritually. This passage challenged me to become a better student of the word of God. I realized that I needed to pray more and become more sensitive to the spiritual needs of others.

I had definitely gotten away from helping other Christians. Verse 13 was a true eye-opener for me. **Hebrews 5:13** *For everyone that useth milk is unskillful* (not capable) *in the word of righteousness: for he is a babe* (new Christian). That verse captured my attention, for I knew that I was not a babe in Christ. I have been saved for many years and after reading that scripture I was spiritually offended. I knew that these verses were written to help mature Christians that were not doing what the Lord desired for us to do.

1Peter 2:2 *As new born babes desire the sincere milk of the word, that ye may grow thereby.*

I was actually just fooling myself until I came into the realization that yes I was saved, but there was so much more that I needed to be doing to lead others to Christ. Satan had me side tracked and at that time I could not lead nor encourage anyone any further than I had gone myself. That was when my spiritual appetite began to grow. I began to feed my inner man; I wanted nothing more to do with being deceived. Satan had slipped one in on me; it is always his desire to get our focus away from others and the things of God. I am so grateful for the love and strength of God and His powerful word.

***2Samuel 22:33** God is my strength and power: he maketh my way perfect.*

God's word is powerful and cuts to the core of all situations.

***Hebrews 4:12** For the word of God is quick, and powerful, and sharper than any twoedged sword, piercing even to the dividing asunder of soul and spirit, and of the joints and marrow, and is a discerner of the thoughts and the intents of the heart.*

We can be deceived in many ways and become convinced that the Lord has forgotten us. It is not uncommon for Christians to live many years believing that the Lord has stopped listening and answering their prayers. That is one of the most popular lies that the devil uses to cause us to give up.

***Hebrews 13:5** Let your conversation be without covetousness; and be content with such things as ye have: for he hath said, I will never leave thee, nor forsake thee.*

This scripture is so important for us to remember, it has so much power within it. It is to be used especially when we get in a slump in our walk with the Lord. The Lord sent His Son Jesus to die for our sins and this verse along with so many others confirm that once He is asked into our hearts, its forever. He does not leave our hearts nor does He leave us physically. We are special to Him and no matter what we do, His love and presence remains.

Unconfessed sins can often cause us to feel disconnected from God and His presence. We may feel as though He is unreachable, but our God is always present and ready to forgive us.

1John 1:9 *If we confess our sins, he is faithful and just to forgive us our sins, and to cleanse us from all unrighteousness.*

Seeking His forgiveness is the ultimate peace that we need and sometimes we also need the forgiveness of others, but the Holy Spirit will also convict our hearts when we need to settled a wrong that we may have done to another person. No matter what the conditions are we do not ever have to be confused of the unconditional love of the Lord. There is absolutely nothing that we cannot be restored from, through Him, except denying His Son.

Matthew 12:31 *Wherefore I say unto you, All manner of sin and blasphemy shall be forgiven unto men: but the blasphemy against the Holy Ghost* (Holy Spirit) *shall not be forgiven unto men.*

As we grow in His word we become stronger and stronger through Him, we are equipped and capable of offering unto others more than the milk of His word. Building our spiritual muscles and bones of course will give us the power and endurance needed to fight off the devil.

There will be times in our spiritual walk that we will get off course and sometimes the devil will lure us in a totally different direction from that which we intend. Physical trainers were not born strong, they at some point had a vision of building a stronger body and once they reached a goal, they began to offer help to others.

We are the same as Christians. The strong are called to help the weak and that can never take place if we do not set the necessary goals. Not even an infant can thrive if they only receive milk for life. We are the same and if we think we can then we are surely fooling ourselves.

To God be the glory for the things that He has done. His word is perfect, simple and exactly what we need to regain focus and to begin to rebuild our spiritual man.

Psalm 19:7 *The law of the Lord is perfect, converting the soul: the testimony of the Lord is sure, making wise the simple.*

If you read this devotion and you never stopped pouring your life into a person then you are to be commended, but if you were just as I was being deceived by the devil there is still hope and time for us.

This was a very hard time in my life because I was not giving and helping when I knew that I should have been. I thank our God because He always grants to us second, third and eternal chances to improve in life.

Let's recommit, the Lord has someone waiting for us to transition from milk to meat spiritually.

Conclusion

God bless your day and I would love to hear your story about the goodness of God in your life. Please send me an email if you feel led to do so.

Email: aretheawrites@gmail.com

Questions to Ponder

Where were you spiritually when you read this devotion?

What one thing did you immediately want to change or keep the same?

What was the name of the most recent person that you encouraged?

Have you continued to pray and encourage them?

Name one thing that you have done consistently since you were saved?

Prayer Request:

Chapter Fifteen

We Will Always Have Haters

John 15:18-19 If the world hate you, ye know that it hated me before it hated you. If you were of the world, the world would love his own: but because ye are not of the world, but I have chosen you out of the world, therefore the world hateth you.

Jesus forewarned us, that we would be hated in this world. Many people live a defeated life because someone or a group of people hate them. David was a great example for us, as he was hated during his time. This is what he said on one account.

Psalm 38:19 *But mine enemies are lively, and they are strong and they that hate me wrongfully are multiplied.*

Psalm 41:7 *All that hate me whisper together against me: against me do they devise my hurt.*

The comfort that we have is knowing that the Lord and His words are there to encourage us each day. One of the deepest hatreds can come from that of a loved one. We may expect the world to display hatred and we are more apt to expect it from them, but never from a loved one.

Christians are more often hated because of the spiritual stand that we take against sinful matters, Jesus reminded us of that in ***John 15: 18-19.***

Here are a few examples in which we may experience hatred during our lifetime: our position in the work place, being the oldest/youngest sibling, enduring a divorce, leading a church ministry, desiring to raise godly children, maintaining higher standards than others etc. These are all means of being hated.

Living life contrary to others beliefs, having a more expensive home/car, wearing nicer clothing - any of these could be reasons to receive hatred from others.

Separating yourself from others, having greater abilities, managing your finances, making Christ Lord of your life, home and finances are additional reasons that others may be compelled to respond with hatred. The list goes on and on and we can all think of so many other reasons why people hate one another. We all have been looked down upon with hatred and for some of us it may very well still exist.

When Jesus told us that we would be hated, He also gave us reasons why and more importantly the proper response to hatred.

Matthew 5:43-44 *Ye have heard that it hath been said, Thou shalt love thy neighbor, and hate thine enemy. But I say unto you, Love your enemies, bless them that curse you, do good to them that hate you, and pray for them which despitefully use you, and persecute you;*

Jesus suffered the ultimate hatred, yet He continued to the cross for our sins. As much as hatred hurts we must endure it as a dear soldier. We must look to Jesus the author and finisher of our faith. We are not to be alarmed when we encounter hatred from our loved ones. Jesus said in **1 John 3:13** *Marvel not, my brethren, if the world hate you.*

We must love and do good to those that hate us, showing more of Christ is always the better way.

Luke 6:27 *But I say unto you which hear, Love your enemies, do good to them which hate you.*

We must guard our hearts so that hatred does not become a part of our lifestyle as well. Know that the Lord shall have revenge in our place.

Romans 12:19 *Dearly beloved, avenge not yourselves, but rather give place unto wrath: for it is written, Vengeance is mine; I will repay, saith the Lord.*

David constantly reminds us that he had many haters as well, we can also draw strength for his pleas to the Lord.

Psalm 69:4 *They that hate me without a cause are more than the hairs of mine head: they that would destroy me, being my enemies wrongfully, are mighty: then I restored that which I took not away.*

When we extend love towards those that hate us as Christians, God says that we are blessed.

Luke 6:22 *Blessed are ye, when men shall hate you, and when they shall separate you from their company, and shall reproach you, cast out your name as evil, for the Son of man's sake.*

Conclusion

Being hated and seeing others hated can be a spiritual challenge. The Lord is concerned with all that we experience in life. He certainly has a reward for our hardships that we endure.

Questions to Ponder:

There are no Questions to Ponder.

Prayer Request:

Chapter Sixteen

Faith During A Funeral

P*salm 116:15 Precious in the sight of the Lord is the death of his saints.*

The bible clearly states that we all will not die; some of us will see the "Rapture" occur.

1Corinthians 15:51-52 Behold, I shew you a mystery; We shall not all sleep, but we shall all be changed, In a moment, in the twinkling of an eye, at the last trump: for the trumpet shall sound and the dead shall be raised incorruptible, and we shall all be changed.

These verses apply to Christians that have accepted the Lord Jesus Christ as their Saviour. Only Christians receive eternal life with God. Has there ever been a time when you realized that you needed a Saviour? Have you asked Him to forgive you of your sins? Have you believed that He died on the cross; was buried and rose again?

Romans 10:9 *That if thou shalt confess with thou mouth the Lord Jesus, and shalt believe in thine heart that God hath raised him from the dead, thou shalt be saved.*

John 3:16 *For God so loved the world, that he gave his only begotten Son, that whosoever believeth in him should not perish, (go to hell) but have everlasting life.*

Eternal life has nothing to do with denominations or the Lord would have recorded it in the bible. They are manmade, not God made.

It's all about being reborn, redeemed, born again, or saved. It depends on the term that we are familiar with, but they all mean the same. We become a new creature in Him and not in man. It is a personal relationship with Christ; it has nothing to do with attending a certain church, although we are to attend church on a regular basis. Salvation can be received anywhere, even outside of the church. It has nothing to do with a certain relative or friend praying us in, it's a personal matter between us and the Lord. We all must be "Born Again".

John 3:3 Jesus answered and said unto him, Verily, verily, I say unto thee, Except a man be born again, he cannot see the kingdom of God.

Salvation does not make the death of a loved one easier to accept, but it does make our last earthly glance of them more comforting, knowing that they are no longer suffering, but are in heaven with the Lord and that one day we will see them again. This is why we must spread the gospel to our family and friends. We can better enjoy our fellowship on earth, when we have the knowledge of peace of eternal life when our lives end. If it were simply according to the works that we've done a great number of people would be in heaven.

It is not about works nor good deeds. Jesus' death on the cross was worth far more than any works that we could have done or do. Helping the elderly and our neighbors are great things that we all should willingly do, but it does not merit us eternal life.

Ephesians 2:8-9 For by grace are ye saved through faith; and that not of yourselves: it is the gift of God: Not of works, lest any man should boast.

This great gift cannot come from man, for man needs salvation as well. God sent His Only Son to pay a sin debt that we could not pay. Knowing that our loved ones and friends are saved gives us a peace and assurance during a funeral. As much as our hearts hurt for their absences we have a sure hope that we will see them again, according to the scriptures.

Attending their funeral allows us to pay our final respects; it also affords us an opportunity to reflect back on their lives and maybe even our relationship with them. At that moment there is nothing that we can do to bring them back or enhance our time spent with them. It is a sad, sorrowful moment even if we have poured ourselves into them.

No one enjoys death even when we witness the failing health of that person; we are still saddened if the Lord chooses to call them home. It seems awkward to be both happy and sad at the same time, but it's okay when we have seen that person lose their quality of life. We can witness and become sensitive to this great scripture that Jesus spoke of about himself and that we can also use in relations to the death of our loved ones.

John 7:33 *Then Jesus said unto them, Yet a little while am I with you and then I go unto him that sent me.*

This verse speaks of Jesus' earthly departure but again, oh how vivid does it describe the departure of a loved one or friend that is a believer.

It has been said that the Lord allows some to see their lives coming to an end, we call it dying grace. One verse that we have quoted is also perfect for saints that are prepared and ready to meet the Lord.

Psalm 23:4 *Yea, though I walk through the valley of the shadow of death, I will fear no evil: for thou art with me; thy rod and thy staff they comfort me.*

The Lord remains present in the lives of both the saved and the unsaved. To the unsaved He bids them to come, and to the saved He desires that we are a witness to others. Hell was not designed for mankind, but those that reject Christ choose to go there. We all enter the world at birth with His "Light" within us. God is not forcible; He wants us to want Him and receive His free gift of eternal life.

John 1:9 That was the true Light, which lighteth everyman that cometh into the world.

John 5:40 And ye will not come to me, that ye might have life.

The word "Eternal Life" appears in 25 verses in the King James Bible

Matthew 19:16;

Matthew 25:46

Mark 10:17

Mark 10:30

Luke 10:25

Luke 18:18

John 4:36

John 5:39

John 6:54

John 6:68

John 12:25

John 17:2-3

Acts 13:48

Romans 2:7

Romans 5:21

Romans 6:23

1 Timothy 6:19

Titus 1:2

Titus 3:7

1 John 1:2

1 John 2:25

1 John 3:15

1 John 5:13

1 John 5:20

Jude 21

Finally, one of the saddest verses recorded.

Revelation 20:15 *And whosoever was not found written in the book of life was cast into the lake of fire.*

Hell is a real place where all unsaved humans will be. The Lord has a better plan for mankind, but we have to willingly except His gift. What a great assurance He gives to those that have trusted in Him, it is called Eternal Life with Him.

John 14:2 *In my Father's house are many mansions: if it were not so, I would have told you. I go to prepare a place for you.*

Faithful assurance during a funeral is what we can embrace when we have to say our final goodbyes. As complicated as it may be, He provides a comforting peace. Here are some words of encouragement.

Conclusion

Thank you for reading this devotion, we all feel empty and at a loss of words when someone dies that we love. Many years ago I wrote this and it has been a blessing to me. I have a more focused view of death and a joy of knowing that through Christ, we will meet again.

Questions to Ponder:

God bless your day, there are no "Questions to Ponder" Just remember that He died that we may live eternally with Him!!!!

Prayer Request:

An Earthly Goodbye

At this gravesite Lord I stand,
as my loved one leaves this land.
My heart is heavy;
my strength is weak.
My faith in you Lord, I shall keep.
As I grieve, from day to day,
guide me Lord, lest I stray.
Death is tragic, and it's hard,
some families grow closer,
while others grow apart.
One sweet minute,
we know not when
the death angel shall appear again.
Someone else will stand in my place,
and have much need, of your comforting grace.
Lord, death can be a blessing and a disappointment too,
especially if the person doesn't know you.
An earthly goodbye we say to the ones that we love,
only salvation can grant them entrance into
your heaven above.

-Arethea M. Green

The End

All books, whether they were good or bad eventually comes to an end. This is the end of this devotional and the final question is, where will you spend eternity? My friend if the Lord was to return right now, or perhaps call you home, will you open your eyes in heaven or hell? I pray that heaven is your answer and that you have a biblical reason why. At any period in your life have you ever realized that you needed a Saviour that is able to secure your eternal state? In John 3:16 The Lord Jesus offers a free eternal gift, Jesus is our only way to heaven. Romans 10:9 tell us that we must call on Him for salvation and 1 John 5:13 assures us of eternal life if we sincerely call upon His name. The Lord has made salvation far simpler than the "Cross." He paid it all there, so that we could freely call upon Him for salvation when we were ready. It would not be comfortable for me to share devotions about Him and not completely introduce Him to my readers. If you have never accepted His free gift, please go back and read the enclosed scriptures when you are ready to respond to His calling on your life. I appreciate your time and would love to hear back from you.

God bless your life and may He be the comfort that you need from day to day.

Arethea Martin Green
Because He Lives, 1 Corinthians 15:58
Email: aretheawrites@gmail.com

Butterfly Beginnings Book Reviews

My first book, *Butterfly Beginnings*, provoked me to reflect on my relationship with Christ, as well as with others for His sake. I'm so thankful that others were blessed by my book and I'd like to share with you some of the comments that were made:

Arethea is sincere and heart felt as she shares her experiences through the Lord. She has grown and desires the same for others. Amen to the word of God that she shares with great passion. **Sheri Boldt**

What an appropriate name for A.M.G.'s first book. Butterfly Beginnings is just a first of many more. Within the pages are devotions form what has moved her as she read the Word of God. They incline interpersonal relationships, personal experiences and things that God has taught her. **Nancy Breen**

I am so proud of my baby sister for writing her first book. It was so unique to read of the goodness of God through her life. **Cynthia Sewell**

Arethea and I share a kindred spirit, which is the love of Christ. I am most proud of my friend and what a great first book. God bless you my friend. **Vicki Dye**

Wow!!! From having taught our child, to becoming the best of friends. Who would have imagined a devotional book to add to our journey? God is good and I am so happy for my friend. **Connie Adams**

We have been friends for many years, the Lord has truly been good to us. We have shared lots of prayer requests and love. It is perfect timing that I could both read and share your book. God bless you my friend, I love you. **Callie Botts**

I am grateful to have many years of close friendship with Arethea. I was quite surprised that I was amongst an author all those years. God bless you and I await your next book, I was blessed through your writing. **Pam Bailey**

The Lord has used many events in our lives to share blessings. For over 30 years as a friend then He allows us to both publish a book together. Only God, Arethea, He has greater coming for us, soon we will be sitting by the water front reflecting. I love you and God bless our writing gift all the more. **Valerie Sutton**

I thank God for allowing our paths to cross, it has been a joy to serve Him with you through the Christian Education of our treasured children. God bless you Arethea, our family loves you. Thank you for writing a great book.
Angela Hylland

A friendship, a blessing and a book, plus many more years of laughter; I pray that the Lord will continue to grant us the privilege to reach children for Him. God bless you, I love you! **Tracy Coffey**

My friend, your book was great, but our friendship is awesome! Thank you for so many years of laughs and prayers. God bless you and please keep writing, it was a blessing to both me and my mom. **Christine Nelson**

Arethea, Michael and I are so blessed to know you and to serve the Lord many years together. Thank you for writing for Him, remember our words "Don't Forget". **Vicky Lishchynsky**

Mrs. Green, we have served the Lord many years together, teaching has been a great highlight of those years. Thank you for sharing your heart in Butterfly Beginnings, Shelby and I truly enjoyed it. God bless you and we love you. **Charlotte Derry**

Oh my! What a joy it has been serving the Lord alongside of you. Reading your book gave me a sense that you were still living in North Carolina. Thank you for using your gift for Him. **Darla Spence**

My friend of 50 years, I am most excited to purchase and read your first book. It has been years of prayers and laughter. A published book is by far the cherry on top of all of God's many blessings in our lives. **Anita Otey**

I remember sitting on the stoop every Saturday in front of my house, when we were only 12 years old; the laughs, the talks, the prayers and now - a second book. Only God. I am so proud of you my friend. **Rosalind Marshall**

Mrs. Green, God bless you and thank you for sharing your

book with us. It was a blessing to serve the Lord with you.
Dianne Covington

For 29 years we have shared an awesome God centered friendship. I thank the Lord for you and for all the years of love and so many good old funny times. I love you my friend. **Yvette Green**

Mrs. Green, God bless you for sharing your heart each day through your book. Our teaching time together was a blessing, thank you for penning a portion of His word, I love you. **Violet Jessie**

Mrs. Green, thank you for sharing your book on the "Free To Be Me Show". It was the Lord that allowed us to meet through Christian Education. Being a part of our family was amazing, we love you and God bless your life.
Pastor Brian Thompson &
Minister Felica Thompson

A Note to My Momma

I thought that by moving to another country, my duties as your typist would end, but that will never be the case will it? You know I don't mind. I am extremely proud of you and both of these honest and inspiring books you've written. Thank you for always being an example and a friend. I love you!

-Anyonita Green-Boyle

Thank You

A special thanks to all of the parents that attended two book signings. I thank the Lord for allowing me to be a small portion of your child's life.

To other family and friends that were not listed please send me your reviews. I promise to use them in upcoming books, may God bless you all and you are loved and prayed for.

Arethea Martin Green

About the Author

I am only a sinner saved by the sweet grace of God.

For many years I had a desire to write and to even have a published book. The Lord used Iris M. Williams, many years after I felt that my dream was gone.

Everyone has a voice that some soul is in need of hearing. Sometimes we have to do things for ourselves before we can be used to encourage someone else.

In the world in which we live, everyone needs a faith lift. Share your story, but give Him alone the glory. The Lord can and desires to use all of us to reach others in areas that we know not of.

My 'book Angel' came into my life on June 16, 2014. Not only did I gain two published books, but a *Godfriend* for life and another reminder that He is not finished with my life.

God bless your life and come on share your story – He has an awesome testimony living inside of you.

Because He lives,

Arethea Martin Green

The Butterfly Typeface Publishing House Co.

The Butterfly Typeface Publishing House Company is a full service professional publishing company. Our goal is to 'spread a message' of inspiration, imagination and intrigue in all that we do.

Whether you hire us to edit, ghostwrite, publish (books & magazines) or web design, you can be guaranteed exemplary customer service, fairness and quality.

Our vision, under God's leadership, is to serve and assist in the healing of the heart, mind and soul of *all* people we encounter with integrity, intentional influence and positive purpose.

"We make good GREAT!"

Iris M. Williams – Owner
The Butterfly Typeface Publishing House Co
Little Rock Arkansas

www.butterflytypeface.com

www.ingramcontent.com/pod-product-compliance
Lightning Source LLC
Chambersburg PA
CBHW071730090426
42738CB00011B/2441